Positive Attitudes at Work

Positive Attitudes at Work

SHARON K. FERRETT

Business Skills Express Series

IRWIN
Professional Publishing

MIRROR PRESS

Burr Ridge, Illinois
New York, New York
Boston, Massachusetts

IRWIN
Concerned About Our Environment

In recognition of the fact that our company is a large end-user of fragile yet replenishable resources, we at IRWIN can assure you that every effort is made to meet or exceed Environmental Protection Agency (EPA) recommendations and requirements for a "greener" workplace.

To preserve these natural assets, a number of environmental policies, both companywide and department-specific, have been implemented. From the use of 50% recycled paper in our textbooks to the printing of promotional materials with recycled stock and soy inks to our office paper recycling program, we are committed to reducing waste and replacing environmentally unsafe products with safer alternatives.

Mirror Press:	David R. Helmstadter
	Carla F. Tishler
Editor-in-chief:	Jeffrey A. Krames
Project editor:	Lynne Basler
Art coordinator:	Mark Malloy
Compositor:	Alexander Graphics, Inc.
Typeface:	12/14 Criterion Book
Printer:	Malloy Lithographing, Inc.

Printed in the United States of America
1 2 3 4 5 6 7 8 9 0 ML 1 0 9 8 7 6 5 4

PREFACE

Attitude is the key to success at work. Employees with positive attitudes are invaluable to the companies of today that have become more and more service-oriented.

As a management consultant, the questions I am asked most often are, "How can I be more positive and enthusiastic at work?" "How can I get others to approach work with a positive attitude?" How can you change your own attitude as well as the attitudes of your co-workers? This book will help you do these things.

The guiding theme of *Positive Attitudes at Work* is that you can empower yourself to create a positive and resourceful state of mind at any time. You also can create a supportive climate where you and your co-workers are inspired to approach work with passion and excitement. As you complete the exercises, you will create a more positive attitude that will enable you to clarify workplace expectations, improve communication, boost morale, and improve productivity.

Sharon K. Ferrett

About the Author

Dr. Sharon Kay Ferrett is the director of the Von Humboldt Scholars Program and professor of management at Humboldt State University in Arcata, California. She is an active consultant in management and self-actualization to private industry and government agencies and has published extensively in those areas. In 1981, Dr. Ferrett was named "Boss of the Year" by the Professional Business Women's Association. She holds a Ph.D. in higher education administration from Michigan State University.

ABOUT IRWIN PROFESSIONAL PUBLISHING

Irwin Professional Publishing is the nation's premier publisher of business books. As a Times Mirror company, we work closely with Times Mirror training organizations, including Zenger-Miller, Inc., Learning International, Inc., and Kaset International to serve the training needs of business and industry.

About the Business Skills Express Series

This expanding series of authoritative, concise, and fast-paced books delivers high-quality training on key business topics at a remarkably affordable cost. The series will help managers, supervisors, and frontline personnel in organizations of all sizes and types hone their business skills while enhancing job performance and career satisfaction.

Business Skills Express books are ideal for employee seminars, independent self-study, on-the-job training, and classroom-based instruction. Express books are also convenient-to-use references at work.

CONTENTS

Self-Assessment

The first step in making change is self-assessment. Assessing your attitude at work will help you create a plan to become more positive and productive. Complete the following questionnaire as honestly as you can.

For each of the statements below, circle the number that most closely reflects your present outlook:

0 = The statement is never true.
1 = The statement is rarely true.
2 = The statement is somewhat true.
3 = The statement is often true.
4 = The statement is always true.

1. I wake up in a good mood.	0 1 2 3 4
2. I look forward to going to work.	0 1 2 3 4
3. I enjoy my job and the work I do.	0 1 2 3 4
4. I feel like I am making a contribution at work.	0 1 2 3 4
5. I like the people I work with and am a team player.	0 1 2 3 4
6. I look at the bright side of situations and people.	0 1 2 3 4
7. I feel secure and confident about my technical and people skills.	0 1 2 3 4
8. I learn from criticism and know when to let it roll off my back.	0 1 2 3 4
9. I can express my emotions without losing control.	0 1 2 3 4
10. I get along well with most people and am well liked.	0 1 2 3 4
11. I have control over my emotions and my state of mind.	0 1 2 3 4
12. I have high energy and enthusiasm.	0 1 2 3 4

13. I have what it takes to take control of my career and my life.   0 1 2 3 4

14. I am eager to grow but comfortable with who I am.   0 1 2 3 4

15. I am able to laugh at my mistakes, learn from them, and then let them go.   0 1 2 3 4

16. I am supportive and happy when others get promoted. I know that there are enough good things in life to go around.   0 1 2 3 4

17. I communicate in a direct, honest, kind, and assertive manner.   0 1 2 3 4

18. I respect myself; I also respect others.   0 1 2 3 4

19. I look forward to learning new skills and taking on more responsibilities at work.   0 1 2 3 4

20. People tend to like me at work.   0 1 2 3 4

21. I am competent, intelligent, attractive, and interesting.   0 1 2 3 4

22. I am comfortable around my superiors.   0 1 2 3 4

23. I am good at creatively solving problems and using critical thinking.   0 1 2 3 4

Add up your total score. If you scored 75 or above, you have an especially positive attitude and self-concept and are modeling this attitude to your co-workers. If your score is under 60, you may want to look at ways to improve your attitude. Your attitude sets the tone for your department and influences your productivity. No matter what your score is, this book will give you insight and direction in improving your attitude.

1 | Attitude: The Key to Success

This chapter will help you to:

- Understand the power of self-image.
- Understand the importance of a positive attitude.
- Review the interrelationship between the mind and body.
- Understand the relationship between needs and attitude.

Sarah Foster has worked at an insurance company for six years and is currently a claims processor. She is a valued employee and has always worked well with others. She has built a reputation of having a positive attitude and being easy to get along with. Sarah has always seen herself as a person who works hard, is result oriented, and follows orders well. She has received several promotions, and recently her boss, Scott Barnes, asked if she would be interested in becoming a supervisor of a large section in the claims division. He gave her a few days to think about it and said they would talk again on Monday. Sarah knows this is a great opportunity, but she wonders if she really has what it takes to be a manager. Before she meets with Scott on Monday, Sarah should think about her self-image, needs, and goals. ∎

1

Questions to Consider

1. What should Sarah do to assess and rethink her self-image, needs, and goals? _____

_____

_____

_____

2. How could she have more confidence and a more positive image of herself? _____

_____

_____

_____

3. If she decides to take the promotion, how can she project a professional image? _____

_____

_____

_____

THE POWER OF SELF-IMAGE

To a large degree you are what you think you are, and you achieve what you think you can. In other words, your behavior is consistent with your self-image. You have a picture of yourself in your head. This image reflects how you feel about yourself and what you think you can accomplish. Your self-image is formed by what you say to yourself and what other people say to you about yourself. Early messages from parents and teachers, experiences with others, and your own self-talk all contributed to your image of yourself. This self-image becomes a powerful force in how you relate to others, what you expect of yourself, and what you achieve—your self-image becomes a self-fulfilling prophecy. What you expect and think you can do is what you will do. So it is important to change your self-image if you want to change your attitude and behavior. Start by looking at your self-image.

■ Exercise 1.1: Self-Image Assessment

1. How would you describe yourself? _____

_____

_____

_____

2. How do you think your co-workers would describe you? _____

_____

_____

_____

3. How would you like others to see you? _____

_____

_____

_____

4. What would be your ideal self? _____

_____

_____

_____

Project a Positive Image

Your self-image determines how other people see you. Some people walk and carry themselves as if they had the hardest job in the world and more responsibility than they can handle. They slouch, sigh, shuffle along, and give the visual image of being overwhelmed and negative. Their clothes look unprofessional and sloppy, they lack a confident walk or posture, and their voices lack enthusiasm. They look like "losers" or like people who are not committed to their professions.

The first step in creating a competent, professional, and confident image is to assess how you come across to others. Take a good honest look at yourself. What does your image say about you?

1

A professional image includes:

- A well-groomed, neat appearance.
- Confident walk and posture.
- Varied and pleasing voice.
- The use of direct eye contact.
- Clean, professional clothing and attire.

Tip

Get feedback. Ask a trusted person who has career experience or ask a career counselor to give you honest feedback about your image, including your posture, walk, voice, and style of eye contact.

THE IMPORTANCE OF A POSITIVE ATTITUDE

Nothing is more important for success in business than a positive attitude. Your attitude can affect everyone's mood and productivity. If you are late to work, feel discouraged about your job, display little enthusiasm, suffer from burnout, or dislike the people you work with, your co-workers will sense this and they may respond with negative attitudes or poor performances. If you are enthusiastic, enjoy your job, look for the best in every situation and in the people you work with, and view problems as an opportunity to grow, your colleagues will want to work with you, will exhibit more enthusiasm, and will show more confidence in you.

The importance of motivated employees with positive attitudes cannot be overstressed in the business world. A positive attitude encourages the following:

- The ability to adapt to change.
- An openness to learning.
- Higher productivity.
- The ability to work with all types of people.
- The ability to learn and grow on the job.
- Creativity in solving problems and seeing solutions.
- The ability to cope with stress.

Define Your Terms

Everyone talks about the importance of a positive attitude, but what exactly is it? People with positive attitudes tend to:

- Have positive feelings about people and situations.
- Have a sense of purpose, excitement, and passion.
- Approach problems in a creative manner.
- Have a resourceful, positive, and enthusiastic air about them.
- Make the best out of every situation.

- Realize that attitude is a choice.
- Feel that they have control of their thoughts.
- Feel that they are making a contribution through their work.

People with a negative attitude, on the other hand, tend to:

- Look at adversity as something that will last forever.
- Feel they are helpless to make a change.
- Focus on the worst that can happen.
- See the negative in people and situations.
- View their state of mind as the result of external factors.
- Feel as if they are victims.
- Approach problems from a win or lose perspective.

Children Have It

Watch a small child and notice the enthusiasm, energy, and spirit of fun. Children live fully in the moment. They explore, seek out new things, smile and laugh, are curious and creative, and approach life with passion. For most children, a positive attitude is a natural state of being. But, along the way, many of us lose this positive attitude. One reason for this loss is the fear of change. Many people either cling to the past or live in the future. They postpone the difficult task of creating positive habits and directly facing and solving daily problems. Instead, they wait for external events to change so that they will be instantly transformed into positive and enthusiastic people. Haven't you heard people say, "When I graduate from school (or have a real job or get married), then I'll be positive, motivated, productive, and enthused about life"?

Life, however, is a series of changes. But, landing the perfect job, making lots of money, attending the best college, or marrying the greatest person in the world will not magically transform you into a motivated and positive person. You must change your attitude first; then your external world will change too.

1

People rarely change their attitudes or habits unless they can see a benefit. Take a few minutes to explore the benefits of a resourceful, positive state of mind. What could you accomplish at work with a more positive attitude?

■ Exercise 1.2: Benefits of a Positive Attitude

Write down the benefits to you, your job, and those around you if you suddenly woke up filled with enthusiasm, motivated to achieve, filled with new ideas, and ready to approach the day with a positive attitude.

_____

_____

_____

_____

THE INTERRELATIONSHIP OF MIND AND BODY

Your body is closely linked to your attitude. When you have a positive attitude, your body reflects this state. An intricate two-way communication system exists between your mind and body. Your attitude affects your immune system, relaxation response, energy level, and overall health. Your body affects your attitude, your emotions, and your mind's ability to handle stress.

Have you ever had the experience of just thinking of speaking in front of a large group? Your heart starts to beat faster, you get butterflies in your stomach, and your palms become sweaty. Similarly, thinking about a loss or unhappy situation can cause you to feel sad and depressed. Conversely, have you ever found that your sadness was lifted by thinking happy thoughts or forcing yourself to smile and laugh?

Being attentive to how your body is feeling and the state of your mind is important in order for change to occur. How observant are you of your body and mind?

1

■ Exercise 1.3: Awareness

Part 1: Sit in a comfortable chair in a quiet space with your feet flat on the floor. Close your eyes and assess your state of mind. Assess your emotional state. Do you like your job, school, relationships, environment, living, and working conditions? Are you angry, upset, worried, resentful, joyous, happy, peaceful, or calm?

Now open your eyes and write as detailed a description as possible of your state of mind. _____

_____

_____

_____

_____

Part 2: Sit in a comfortable chair in a quiet space with your feet flat on the floor. Close your eyes and assess your physical state. Then open your eyes and write an assessment of your physical state:

_____

_____

_____

Are you experiencing any discomfort?

Are you experiencing pain?

Are you experiencing stiffness?

Are your shoulders tight?

Is your jaw tight?

Generally speaking:

Do you suffer from headaches?

Do you suffer from backaches?

Do you sleep well?

Do you exercise regularly?

Do you take any drugs to sleep?

Do you smoke or drink alcohol?

Is your weight where you want it to be?

Do you come home from work exhausted?

Do you have lots of energy?

Cycle of Success

Your self-image (your beliefs and attitude about yourself) influences what you say to yourself (self-talk), which in turn influences your body (breathing, muscular tension, posture, blushing). Such physical reactions influence your behavior (actions, verbal responses). This cycle is illustrated below.

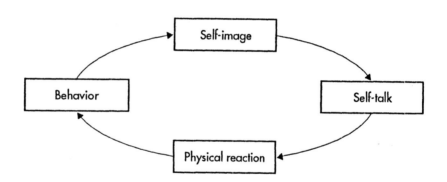

Tip ──────────────────────────────────

Observe successful people or read biographies of famous people or successful people in your field. How did their attitudes contribute to their successes? Talk with people who have lived through the Great Depression, severe loss, illness, or personal tragedy. Ask how their attitudes helped them get through these difficult times. Observe co-workers whom you admire. What kinds of attitude do they have? Jot down similar traits from your readings and observations.

1

NEEDS AND ATTITUDE

Over three decades ago, Abraham H. Maslow,[1] a noted psychologist, and Frederick Herzberg,[2] a noted management theorist, studied needs and the relationship between needs, motivation, and attitudes. Although their research is too exhaustive to discuss thoroughly here, we can draw some conclusions from their work about needs and attitudes.

People often try to change their attitudes by focusing on their lower-level needs. For example, "If only I had more money, a bigger office, or nicer co-workers, then I'd be satisfied and productive." But it requires more to create a positive attitude than simply to satisfy low-level needs such as salary, benefits, working conditions, job security, and company rules. Although these needs are important and can result in dissatisfaction when they are missing, when they are maintained, they do not necessarily satisfy or motivate us. Higher needs—achievement, recognition, growth, responsibility, power, and accomplishment—are more likely to motivate you in the long run.

Once basic needs are met, long-lasting motivation comes from a sense of purpose and is driven by these higher-order needs. The driving force that influences your attitude and causes you to be positive, truly motivated, and passionate about your work comes from within. Some people have a driving need for power, to find truth, to create beauty, to promote justice, to excel, and to achieve. The one need that seems to be universal and fundamental is the need to be recognized and feel important.

How do you make yourself feel valued and important at work? How do you help your co-workers feel valued and important?

---

[1] Abraham H. Maslow, *Motivation and Personality*, 2nd ed. (New York: Harper & Row, 1970).

[2] Frederick Herzberg, B. Mausner, and Barbara Snyderman, *The Motivation to Work*, 2nd ed. (New York: Wiley, 1959).

Assess Your Needs Periodically

No simple solution exists for magically transforming your attitude. Nevertheless, it is helpful to analyze your needs to see how they affect your attitude and motivate you to act.

■ Exercise 1.4: Needs Assessment

1. What needs are most important in your life at this time? Which needs relate to your work? _____

   _____

   _____

   _____

2. If you had all the money you needed to pay your bills, but were still required to make a positive contribution to life, what would you do for a career? _____

   _____

   _____

   _____

3. In what ways can you meet the higher-level needs of achievement, recognition, and self-actualization in your present job? _____

   _____

   _____

   _____

Chapter 1 Checkpoints

✓ Your self-image reflects how you feel about yourself and is formed by what you say about yourself and what others say about you.

✓ A positive attitude will help you to:
> Accomplish your goals.
> Adapt to change.
> Be open to learning.
> Be more productive.
> Work effectively with others.
> Solve problems in a creative way.
> Cope with stress.

✓ Your attitude affects your body's immune system, energy level, ability to relax, and overall health.

✓ The most fundamental human need is the need to feel important.

2 | Types of Work Attitudes

This chapter will help you to: ————————————

- Identify types of positive attitudes.
- Identify types of negative attitudes.
- Determine the attitude types of your co-workers.

Mario Baneño has worked with mentally retarded people for 12 years in a small school system. Mario has earned a reputation for being hard working, caring, and a perfectionist. Recently he was promoted to department supervisor. He has always found his work to be extremely rewarding and has worked hard to get along with everyone on his staff. In his new position, Mario works with a variety of people—teachers, staff, administrators, trustees, parents, and social workers. Mario must work with several difficult people, but he has never assessed why he finds them difficult. He has simply tried to avoid them. But, as a supervisor, he must now learn to work effectively with these people.

Karen Cartwright, a co-worker, is a case in point. She and Mario have always rubbed each other the wrong way. Recently, they were assigned to a project together. Karen has a laid-back attitude that annoys the perfectionist in Mario. Yesterday, she came to a meeting late and tried to push through her project before doing her homework. Mario reacted angrily and said a few harsh words, which he quickly regretted. He has a meeting with her today and wants to start fresh. ■

Questions to Consider

1. What would you suggest to Mario to help him prepare for this meeting? _____
_____
_____
_____

2. How can Mario get to know his staff and co-workers better?
_____
_____
_____

3. What would you suggest to Mario to help him work with Karen on this project? _____
_____
_____
_____

In any organization, there are work attitudes that are supportive and positive and attitudes that are destructive and negative. Supportive attitudes validate and increase your sense of self-esteem.

Exercise 2.1: Positive Attitudes

1. Identify two people with whom you like to work. _____
_____
_____

2. What specific traits make these people enjoyable to work with?
_____
_____

3. What specific feelings do you experience when you are with each person? _____
_____
_____

POSITIVE WORK ATTITUDES

There are at least six positive attitudes that can validate and increase your sense of worth. These six positive work attitudes also can transform the workplace into a productive and positive environment.

The Willing-to-Learn Attitude

A person with a willing-to-learn attitude:

- Is open to new ideas.
- Listens actively and patiently.
- Asks relevant questions.
- Isn't a know-it-all on every subject.
- Seeks out advice.
- Empathizes with other people's viewpoints.
- Continually upgrades his or her job skills.
- Takes seminars in human-relations skills.
- Takes on new job responsibilities.
- Believes that learning is a lifelong process.

Co-workers say that working with a person who has a willing-to-learn attitude makes them feel interesting, valued, and informed.

The Take-Charge Attitude

A person with a take-charge attitude:

- Takes charge of situations.
- Takes full responsibility for his or her attitude and actions.
- Looks for solutions.
- Feels empowered to take control and make sound decisions.
- Refuses to be a victim of circumstances or events.
- Does not wait for life to change.

2

- Makes his or her own luck.
- Explores options.
- Has a good sense of humor.

Co-workers like working with a person who has a take-charge attitude. They enjoy this person's sense of direction and energy.

The Involved Attitude

A person with an involved attitude:

- Is interested in getting the job done.
- Takes an active role in projects and meetings.
- Is a valued team member.
- Offers alternatives for solving problems.
- Is enthusiastic and has a love of life.
- Uses critical thinking to weigh decisions.
- Does not take long to make a choice.
- Does not look back once a choice is made.

Co-workers enjoy being around a person who is vital and full of life.

The Assertive Attitude

A person with an assertive attitude:

- Is calm and confident.
- Is direct and aboveboard with concerns.
- Is problem centered.
- Uses direct eye contact.
- Has confident body language.
- Uses gestures that are congruent with his or her tone of voice and use of language.
- Delivers a message that is clear, concise, and direct.

- Goes directly to the source of a problem.
- Refuses to gossip or criticize others behind their backs.

Co-workers say they always know where they stand with this person. They appreciate the professional attitude and the fair, kind, and tactful style.

The Positive Attitude

A person with a positive attitude:

- Is upbeat, focused, and cheerful.
- Looks at the possibilities and the bright side of every situation.
- Sees problems as opportunities and challenges.
- Likes to explore options.
- Is enthusiastic and productive.
- Brings a sense of joy to work.
- Is optimistic and hopeful.

Co-workers enjoy working with positive people and say that their optimism is contagious and fun.

The Supportive Attitude

A person with a supportive attitude:

- Listens intently.
- Shows empathy and concern.
- Is sensitive and tactful.
- Is able to express feelings and emotions.
- Is receptive and supportive.
- Is approachable.
- Brings a sense of harmony to the workplace.

Co-workers find the supportive person open to new ideas, supportive of their views, and always willing to listen.

■ Exercise 2.2: Recognizing Positive Attitudes

1. Have you ever worked with people who have any of the positive work attitudes described above? If so, describe your experiences with them and how you felt working with these types of people.

_____

_____

_____

2. Are there other work attitudes that you find effective? Describe them here. _____

_____

_____

_____

■ Tip

Use praise often and reward positive attitudes. Search out positive attitudes and behaviors, and let people know you appreciate them. People respond to spontaneous praise or compliments more than to a comment at a yearly performance review.

NEGATIVE WORK ATTITUDES

Just as positive work attitudes validate others and create a supportive work climate, negative attitudes invalidate others and create a destructive work climate. Here are a few negative work attitudes:

The Expert Attitude

A person with an expert attitude:

- Is a know-it-all.
- Acts superior and condescending.
- Tries to impose views on everyone.

- Always has an opinion on every subject.
- States a viewpoint as fact.
- Gives not only an answer but *the* answer to every situation.
- Has an arrogant tone of voice and posture.

Co-workers complain that when they are around "experts," they feel inferior, uninformed, and even stupid.

The Whiner Attitude

A person with a whiner attitude:

- Complains about everything.
- Sees life as unfair.
- Refuses to accept any responsibility.
- Blames others or the system.
- Constantly whines about how awful life is.
- Feels powerless to take control of his or her life.
- Does not want to find solutions to problems.
- Wants sympathy or for someone else to fix problems.
- Feels that others have a much easier life.
- Feels unlucky.

Whiners make co-workers feel guilty and frustrated. Although co-workers offer them suggestions, they are rarely followed. They often end up helping out the whiner and doing more than their share of the work.

The Passive Attitude

A person with a passive attitude:

- Is withdrawn.
- Refuses to participate or contribute.
- Rarely voices an opinion or takes a stand on an issue.

- Does not want to rock the boat or create any conflict.
- Goes along with what others want.
- Shows little enthusiasm for life.
- Does not use creativity in solving problems.
- Often has trouble making even simple decisions.
- Says yes to unwanted requests.
- Sometimes does not follow through on projects.

Co-workers complain that they are forced to make all the decisions and feel they are being cheated out of the passive person's views, ideas, and thoughts.

The Attacker Attitude

A person with an attacker attitude:

- Likes to criticize and belittle others.
- Snipes at people in groups.
- Talks behind others' backs.
- Sometimes explodes in anger.
- Uses jokes or sarcasm as a way to put others down.
- Is moody.
- Can be entertaining, outgoing, and fun one minute and the next make very hurtful comments.
- Often says that others are too sensitive or can't take a joke.

Co-workers complain that they feel intimidated and bullied when they are around an attacker.

The Negative Attitude

A person with a negative attitude:

- Tends to analyze every detail.
- Focuses on the negative in every situation.

- Sees obstacles as overwhelming barriers.
- Is a wet blanket to any new idea.
- Uses phrases such as, "This will never work," or "We've tried this already."
- Has a negative tone of voice and closed body language.

Co-workers complain that people with negative attitudes drag them down with their lack of enthusiasm and their dark view of life.

The Controlling Attitude

A person with a controlling attitude:

- Acts in a manipulative manner.
- Focuses on his or her preferred outcome.
- Disregards others' feelings or suggestions.
- Likes to control situations.
- Likes to shake things up.
- Wants to win at any cost.
- Comes across as overwhelming.
- Has a strong voice and direct gestures.
- Interrupts people.
- Has forceful ideas.

Co-workers often feel intimidated and bullied around a controlling person. Sometimes they feel as if the controller has a hidden agenda.

2

■ Exercise 2.3: Recognizing Negative Attitudes

1. Have you ever worked with people who have any of the negative work attitudes described above? If so, describe your experiences with them and how you felt working with these types of people.

_____

_____

_____

2. Are there other work attitudes that you find ineffective? Describe them here: _____

_____

_____

_____

■ Tip

Actively listen to your co-workers, and let them know that you are really interested in them. Build time into your work schedule for this camaraderie and office friendship. Do more listening than talking. What are the concerns of your co-workers? What motivates them?

DETERMINE THE ATTITUDE TYPES OF CO-WORKERS

If your co-workers were to take an attitude test and wear their labels on a button, you could work with them more effectively. No one, of course, falls neatly into one category, and moods and situations can affect attitude. Through observation, however, you can identify patterns of behavior, and you will come to see that most co-workers fall into general categories.

Although your purpose is not to stereotype your co-workers, categorizing them will give you insight to identify appropriate strategies to work with them more effectively, as you will see in Chapter 3.

■ Exercise 2.4: Observation

Observe the people you work with. What attitude categories do they fall into? How do you think you could work with these people more effectively?

Name   *Attitude*

_____   _____

_____   _____

_____   _____

_____   _____

_____   _____

_____   _____

Chapter 2 Checkpoints

✓ Positive work attitudes can increase productivity and create a supportive work climate. Positive work attitudes include:

    Willing-to-learn attitude.
    Take-charge attitude.
    Involved attitude.
    Assertive attitude.
    Positive attitude.
    Supportive attitude.

✓ Negative work attitudes can result in lower morale and productivity and create a destructive work climate. Negative work attitudes include:

    Expert attitude.
    Whiner attitude.
    Passive attitude.
    Attacker attitude.
    Negative attitude.
    Controlling attitude.

3 | Dealing with Negative Attitudes

This chapter will help you to:

- Review the six types of negative attitudes in detail.
- Explore specific strategies for dealing effectively with negative attitudes.
- Consider general and specific strategies for overcoming your negative attitudes.
- Identify positive traits of negative people.

Carlos Bermedeas is a paralegal in a large law firm. He is intelligent and has always been a hard worker. During college, he had to work full time, so he had little time to socialize. He spent most of his time studying or working. He gave little thought to getting along with others before he started his career. Now that he works full time, Carlos realizes that building relationships is a big part of his job. Sometimes he feels inadequate dealing with co-workers, especially Angela Cortez, his supervisor. She rarely listens to his concerns or suggestions. Carlos finds Angela's attitude to be controlling and demanding. He is often asked to work through lunch or overtime with little warning.

In the past few months, Carlos has become increasingly frustrated and feels he has lost control of his life. He feels invalidated, but does not know what he should do. Next Tuesday he has his performance review with Angela and wants to discuss his goal of improving their working relationship. ■

Questions to Consider

1. What should Carlos do to plan for this meeting? _____

_____

_____

_____

2. How can Carlos create a positive working relationship with Angela?

_____

_____

_____

3. How can Carlos gain more control over his time and his job?

_____

_____

_____

Chapter 2 identified several common negative attitudes. These attitudes invalidate others and can result in a destructive and unproductive work environment. Now that you know how to recognize negative, invalidating attitudes, you can learn to defuse and cope with them.

■ Exercise 3.1: Negative Attitudes

1. Identify two people with whom you do not like to work. _____

_____

_____

2. What specific traits make these people unpleasant to work with?

_____

_____

3. What specific feelings do you experience when you are with each of these people? _____

_____

_____

Look at the following examples of negative attitudes. How would you deal with these people? Feel free to add to the following suggestions for diverting and managing negative attitudes in others and in yourself.

THE EXPERT

Jay Goldstein is a computer programmer at a software company and is working with DeAnn Longtine on a major project. DeAnn has had some experience working on a similar project at another company. Over the weekend, DeAnn sketched out a proposal for the new project and took it to Jay on Monday morning. He rolled his eyes and in a condescending tone told her that this was not the correct approach. He knows it would never work because marketing computer programs is his area of expertise. DeAnn feels invalidated and put down. ∎

1. Imagine that you are Jay's co-worker. What would you do to create a better working relationship? _____
   _____
   _____

2. Write a short script for DeAnn to follow the next time Jay dismisses her ideas.
   _____
   _____
   _____
   _____

3

Specific Strategies

Here are a few specific suggestions for working more effectively with an expert (in this case, Jay):

1. Be prepared and state the facts. Have the latest information. Refer to authorities. If you have solid information, quote your sources. Ask Jay why he is resisting new factual information.

2. Ask detailed questions. "How would you apply that concept to our project? Please go into more detail, Jay."

3. Never argue or challenge. Make clear, concise, and factual statements and ask questions. "Where did you hear that figure, Jay?"

4. Actively listen. Respect the expert's views and paraphrase back to him what you heard. Don't interrupt. "Jay, did I understand you to say that production fell last term by 50 percent?"

5. Be respectful and tolerant. Model integrity by being respectful, tolerant, and logical. Don't be counterproductive by trying to prove that you are right or by being dogmatic. Indicate that you appreciate his knowledge and experience.

6. Acknowledge different viewpoints. Concede that you see the situation differently and that you are willing to listen to different viewpoints. In other words, let Jay be the expert.

7. Don't paint the expert into a corner. Leave the expert room to save face. "Jay, I appreciate your experience and knowledge. Before you use that figure, would you get an up-to-date source just to double check?"

When the Expert Is You

If you have an expert attitude at times, try to:

1. Listen more and ask questions.

2. Admit that you don't have all the answers.

3. Practice saying, "I don't know," when it's appropriate.

4. Be open minded rather than dogmatic.

5. Develop the ability to apologize or say, "I was wrong."

THE WHINER

Gail White is a medical technician in a hospital. She likes her job and has good technical skills but seems to have problems taking control of her career and her personal life. She has even talked about quitting and finding a higher-paying job. She works with Ben Rich, and they share office space. This morning Gail went into great detail about how awful her life was. She just received a less-than-glowing performance review, her boyfriend had just broken up with her, she can't seem to save money, and her landlady has raised the rent. In addition, she dislikes working with a fellow co-worker and complains of how unfair it is that she does so much work in the lab and receives so little recognition. Ben feels depressed after listening to Gail but doesn't want to be rude or unkind. What should he do? ∎

1. Imagine you are Gail's co-worker. What would you do to create a better working relationship with her? _____

_____

_____

2. Write out a short script for Ben to follow the next time Gail starts to unload on him.

_____

_____

_____

_____

3

Specific Strategies

Here are a few specific suggestions for working more effectively with a whiner (in this case, Gail):

1. **Clarify the purpose.** In a tactful way, ask what she wants from you. "Gail, do you want my suggestions, or do you just want to talk and let off steam?"

2. **Actively listen and paraphrase back.** "Gail, you have had a bad day."

3. **Acknowledge the whiner's feelings.** "Gail, it sounds as if you feel overwhelmed."

4. **Ask questions.** "Do you really want to quit your job, Gail?"

5. **Ask for alternatives.** Don't give advice unless asked for. "Gail, what alternatives have you considered besides quitting your job?"

6. **Ask for specific results.** "Gail, if this could turn out the way you want it, what would you want from this situation?"

When the Whiner Is You

If you have a whining attitude at times, try to:

1. Deal with solutions and alternatives, not barriers.
2. Learn to see problems as challenges and opportunities for growth.
3. Remember that everyone has to deal with setbacks and problems.
4. Tell yourself that you can cope with any problem that occurs.
5. Get into an active rather than a complaining mode.

THE PASSIVE PERSON

Bob Green is a graphic artist for a large furniture company. For years he could quietly hide as he competently performed his job. But then the company went through a major reorganization. His new supervisor, Hillary Duran, has created work teams. Now

Bob must meet on a regular basis with co-workers from across the company. Hillary is becoming frustrated with Bob's passive behavior. At this morning's meeting, Bob was quiet and withdrawn and would not give suggestions when asked for his ideas. What should Hillary do? ■

3

1. Imagine that you are Bob's co-worker. What would you do to create a better working relationship? _____
_____
_____

2. Write out a short script for Hillary to use the next time Bob clams up.

_____
_____
_____
_____

Specific Strategies

Here are a few specific suggestions for working with a passive person (in this case, Bob):

1. **Describe the behavior.** "Bob, you haven't given us your opinion and you have been very quiet."
2. **State what you want.** "Bob, it is important that we have your viewpoint on this project."
3. **Ask for a commitment.** "Would you agree, Bob, to have that section completed by Wednesday at 3:00 in the afternoon?"
4. **Ask questions.** "Bob, explain in more detail what it was like to work on the Murry project. What were the problems involved?"
5. **Use direct eye contact.**
6. **Put the passive person in charge.** "Bob, I'd like you to present the opening remarks to the sales department."

3

When the Passive Person Is You

If you have a passive attitude at times, try to:

1. Ask more questions and get involved.
2. Focus on the situation and others rather than on your own feelings.
3. Voice your concerns and opinions.
4. Speak up and use direct eye contact.
5. See the fun in life and be able to laugh at yourself.
6. Get action oriented and pretend that you are the leader.

> ■ **Tip** ─────────────────────────
> Call a staff meeting for a two-hour break in the afternoon. Have really good refreshments and create a fun atmosphere. Have staff draw a description of a negative attitude out of a hat and practice roleplaying different responses and writing effective scripts.

THE ATTACKER

Beth Gray angrily approached Maureen Harris in the hallway of their real estate office on Monday morning. Beth shouted accusations and demanded to know why Maureen had taken a client out to dinner on Friday, when Beth had already made plans to go out for a drink with the same client. As real estate associates, Beth and Maureen often dined together, shared a secretary, and covered for each other during vacations. Maureen enjoys Beth, respects her competency, but dislikes her temper. One minute Beth can be witty and fun and the next, biting and explosive.

Beth went on to accuse Maureen of stealing her client and of wearing unprofessional clothes; she then took a detour and questioned Maureen's budget figures. ■

1. Imagine that you are Beth's co-worker. What would you do to create a better working relationship? _____

   _____

   _____

2. Write a short script for Maureen to follow the next time Beth blows up at her.

   _____

   _____

   _____

   _____

Specific Strategies

Here are a few specific suggestions for working more effectively with an attacker (in this case, Beth):

1. **Stay calm.** Keep your voice low, calm, and even. Look the attacker directly in the eye. "Beth, I'd like to hear what you're saying, but you are speaking too loudly."

2. **Express your feelings.** "Beth, that remark was a dig. It was insulting, and I feel angry."

3. **Use confident body language.** Stand tall and confident. Don't giggle, smile, or make use of sarcasm or jokes.

4. **Focus on the problem.** Don't get detoured. "Beth, we were discussing a real estate client, not my clothes."

5. **Ask for a private meeting.** "Beth, this is not the place to discuss my budget figures. Let's meet in my office."

When the Attacker Is You

If you have an attacking attitude at times, try to:

1. Take a deep breath and think before you spout off.
2. Control your emotions and behavior.
3. Look for win/win solutions.
4. Be assertive while being kind, tactful, and respectful.
5. See the situation from the other person's point of view.
6. Focus on the problem and not the personality.

Tip

Recognize and celebrate differences. When you expect others to feel, think, act, and work like you do, you set yourself up for disappointment. Withhold judgment and recognize that people have different strengths and approaches to solving problems. Learn to use and applaud these different styles. Once you start to see people from a point of appreciation, you will notice that ideas flow and more effective decisions can be made.

THE NEGATIVIST

Thomas Minton is a sales representative in a large telecommunications company. He has worked there for several years and is a supervisor in the sales department. The company has recently gone through a complete reorganization, and Thomas was not chosen for district supervisor. This has been bothering him. Judy Ang is the supervisor for the marketing division and works closely with Thomas. She knows that he was hoping for the promotion, but wonders if his failure to get it isn't somehow related to his negative attitude. While competent, Thomas has a tendency to look for the worst in every situation. He rarely says anything positive. Others have complained about his attitude, and Judy agrees that it creates an unproductive climate. She has often started a meeting only to find that Thomas's negative attitude brings her down. She is preparing for a meeting with him to discuss the company's account with the Keiser Corporation, and she wants the meeting to be productive. She knows that in the past Thomas has asserted that servicing this account requires too much time and has nothing to offer the company. What can she do? ■

3

1. Imagine that you are Thomas's co-worker. What would you do to create a better working relationship with him? _____

   _____

   _____

   _____

2. Write a short script to follow the next time Thomas starts with his gloom and doom.

   _____

   _____

   _____

   _____

Specific Strategies

Here are a few specific suggestions for working more effectively with a negativist (in this case, Thomas):

1. **Remain optimistic.** Remind yourself that you choose your attitude; don't be influenced by another person's negative one.
2. **State your optimistic viewpoint.** Don't be unrealistic or compensate by being too sunny. "Thomas, I believe there are several good things about taking on the Keiser project."
3. **Actively listen.** Paraphrase back to the negativist. Don't argue. Respect his point of view and don't try to talk him out of it.

4. **Ask for alternatives and solutions.** Get the negativist to list possibilities. "Thomas, what are the alternatives to turning down the project? Could we add overtime?"

5. **Take action independently.** If possible, move ahead on your own. "I understand, Thomas, that you have reservations about the project. I will work with Jason on it, however, because I think it has real merit."

When the Negativist Is You

If you have a negative attitude at times, try to:

1. Learn to look at the positive in the situation.
2. Ask others about the upside of the situation.
3. Point out potential concerns without being negative.
4. Focus on solutions rather than problems.
5. Look squarely at the worst that could happen. Is this likely?

THE CONTROLLER

Wendy Chinn has just had an argument with her co-worker Brad Fisher. Wendy and Brad are both engineers in an environmental water resource company and work on the same project team. Wendy is puzzled by Brad's reaction to her proposal that they take the Doons project instead of the Ocean project. The Doons project would add much more visibility to their company and open up doors for bigger projects. She did consider talking to him before she submitted her proposal, but decided there was no reason to delay it. Wendy sent in the proposal without Brad's approval or signature and made plans for her—not him—to present it at a major meeting.

When Brad voiced his objections to her proposal, Wendy cut him off before he could finish. She became loud and spoke very fast, not letting Brad get a word in.

Wendy will admit that she is very forceful and can be overbearing, but she argues that the same force has helped her take control of her education and career. Brad understands and admires Wendy's drive, but feels she goes too far to push her ideas and control. What should he do? ■

3

1. Imagine you are Wendy's co-worker. What would you do to create a better working relationship? _____

_____

_____

2. Write a short script for Brad to follow the next time Wendy tries to control him.

_____

_____

_____

_____

Specific Strategies

Here are a few specific suggestions for working more effectively with a person who has a controlling attitude (in this case, Wendy):

1. **Stand up.** Look directly at her. Speak in a low and direct voice. "Wendy, I expect you to clear decisions with me first before acting independently."
2. **Don't argue.** Be firm. "This is a team project."
3. **Make your points clearly and forcefully.** Don't fight. "Wendy, I expect to co-sign all proposals."
4. **Ask for the controller's objections.** "Wendy, tell me more about your concerns about my giving the presentation."
5. **Calm her down.** "I want to hear your points, Wendy, but you are speaking too loud and too fast. Please calm down."

6. **Demand respect.** "Wendy, you interrupted me. Please allow me to finish my point."

7. **Find common ground.** "We both want the project to be successful. Let's compromise on who does the presentation."

8. **Get an agreement.** "In the future, Wendy, will you agree to discuss the proposals first before you make independent decisions?"

When the Controller Is You

If you have a controlling attitude at times, try to:

1. Ask for other people's opinions, suggestions, and viewpoints.

2. Get others involved in problem solving and presentation.

3. Listen. Don't express your opinion too soon.

4. Allow others to be responsible for their tasks.

5. Read body language. Make certain you are sensitive to the feelings of others in addition to focusing your attention on getting the job done.

GENERAL STRATEGIES

Here is a list of general ways to diffuse difficult attitudes before they become a real problem:

1. **Assess and face each situation directly.** Determine if the difficult situation represents a pattern of behavior or is an isolated incident. Try to understand what attitude it reflects. Acknowledge and accept the person rather than hope for change, excuse the behavior, or ignore the problem.

2. **Actively listen to the other person.** Don't interrupt or get angry. Pause and listen to the other person's viewpoint. Paraphrase what the other person has said.

3. Express your feelings from your own point of view. Use "I" when describing your feelings. "I feel resentful when you don't contribute your ideas," rather than, "You make me feel . . ."

4. Describe the situation in a clear, concise manner. In a sentence or two, describe the other person's behavior. Focus on the behavior and the attitude, not the person. For example, "Jean, that was a hurtful remark" rather than "Jean, you are so rude."

5. State what you want. In a direct and assertive manner, state what you want from the other person. For example, "John, I want you to follow up on your commitment and complete Part 1 of the report."

6. Practice. Rehearse your response, and mentally see yourself behaving in a calm, direct, and assertive manner. If you do not respond with integrity, review the situation and practice responding correctly. Your goal is not to change the other person, but to act honestly, with integrity and respect.

Exercise 3.2: Monitor the Results

Recall a recent encounter with a co-worker who exhibited one of the destructive attitudes described above:

1. Briefly describe the encounter. _____
_____
_____

2. Describe how you dealt with this person. _____
_____
_____

3. What results did you achieve? _____
_____
_____

4. If you could relive this encounter, how would you modify your approach? _____
_____
_____

When All Else Fails

When your best efforts to defuse a difficult attitude have failed and you must work with a difficult person, try some of these general strategies:

1. **Inquire.** Ask if something is wrong or if the person meant to insult you. Get him or her talking.
2. **Confront.** Point out the person's destructive attitude and behavior and his or her resistance to harmony.
3. **Express your feelings.** Explain how the person is invalidating you and how you feel about it.
4. **Reflect.** Is there some truth in what the person is saying, even if it is not said tactfully?
5. **Stand your ground.** Focus on the facts.
6. **Mediate.** Bring in a third party to help you communicate better.
7. **Take a break.** Talking about something neutral or taking a walk can give you some needed distance. You might simply nod and say, "Yes, I see."
8. **Reframe.** See this person as a challenge. Say to yourself, "This person helps me practice my skills."
9. **Use humor.** Poke fun at yourself and the situation and don't take every comment personally or get emotionally involved.
10. **Gain perspective.** Consider the source. If this person has a reputation for being difficult, his or her comments and behavior may have nothing to do with you.

Of course, you can withdraw and not work with or be around someone who constantly invalidates you. But avoidance is a last resort. When you must work with someone, do it with dignity; remind yourself of your sense of worth and confidence.

Focus on the Positive

Everyone has different strengths and weaknesses. A person with a negative work attitude also has a positive side. We tend to like people who are similar to us, but a different style and attitude can be helpful in forming an effective work team. Focus on some of the positive traits that a person with a negative work attitude might have and how valuable these could be in a work situation. Here are a few possibilities:

Experts tend to:

- Like detail.
- Think clearly.
- Act methodically.
- Be cautious.

Whiners tend to:

- Like people.
- Be sensitive.
- Like accuracy.

Passive persons tend to:

- Listen.
- Follow directions.
- Value loyalty.

Attackers tend to:

- Get involved.
- Like action.
- Be spirited and fun.

Negativists tend to:

- See the barriers.
- Want accuracy.
- Show patience.

Controllers tend to:

- Take charge.
- Get results.
- Organize and solve problems.

3

Chapter 3 Checkpoints

✓ When working with the expert attitude, be prepared and state the facts.

✓ When working with the whiner attitude, listen actively and paraphrase messages.

✓ When working with the passive attitude, ask for ideas and get a commitment.

✓ When working with the attacker attitude, stay calm and problem centered.

✓ When working with the negative attitude, be optimistic and explore options.

✓ When working with the controller attitude, state concerns and points clearly and forcefully.

4 | Barriers to Positive Work Attitudes

This chapter will help you to:

- Identify the factors that contribute to positive and negative work attitudes.
- Overcome low self-esteem.
- Recognize and overcome fears of failure and success.
- Recognize and learn strategies to overcome career plateaus.
- Recognize and learn strategies to overcome faulty perception.

Jack Berkovitz joined a software company right after college. Bright, competent, and hardworking, he advanced quickly and earned several promotions. He was soon supervising others. However, the company has been downsizing, and there have been many layoffs. In addition, many perks have been cut, there are few advancement opportunities, and there have been no raises for two years. Employee morale is low, and several co-workers have negative and unproductive work attitudes. Jack has also felt discouraged and finds it difficult to maintain a positive attitude at this time.

Jack wants to plan some programs to encourage positive work attitudes both for himself and for his staff. ■

4

Questions to Consider

1. What strategies would help Jack and his staff create and maintain a positive attitude? _____
_____
_____
_____

2. What can Jack do to increase the confidence and sense of self-worth of his co-workers? _____
_____
_____
_____

CONTRIBUTING FACTORS

Employees can be dissatisfied, unproductive, and have negative attitudes for many reasons. Some reasons are work-related and others may involve their personal lives. It is important to look at barriers to positive work attitudes and explore ways to overcome them.

■ Exercise 4.1: Negative Attitudes

Think back to a time when you were particularly negative and had an unproductive attitude. Perhaps you could hardly drag yourself out of bed. List the factors that contributed to your lack of enthusiasm and poor performance. Describe your emotions, your state of mind, and how you felt and behaved physically:

_____
_____
_____

Compare your list with these common negative external and internal factors:

A dreary office can be a drain on positive attitude.

Negative External Factors

1. Climate that is too cold, hot, dreary, or rainy.
2. Poor economy.
3. Little team support or cooperation.
4. An unattractive work environment.
5. Low morale and unsupportive corporate culture.
6. Low salary.
7. Unsafe conditions.
8. Rigid job description.

Negative Internal Factors

1. Hopelessness and helplessness.
2. Low self-esteem.
3. Fear of failure.
4. Seeing the worst possible outcome.
5. Little recognition or chance of achievement.

6. Learning disability.

7. Depression or emotional difficulties.

8. Resentment.

■ Exercise 4.2: Positive Attitudes

Think back to a time when you were really positive. You may have been involved in a sport, a school play, a new job, or a challenging activity. You were enthused and committed to give it your best. What factors influenced your attitude and performance? Describe your emotions, your state of mind, and how you felt and acted. _____

_____

_____

_____

Compare your list with these common positive external and internal factors:

Positive External Factors

1. A new and varied job.

2. Learning new job skills.

3. Working in a pleasant environment.

4. Being part of a team.

5. Having flexibility and freedom to make decisions.

6. Doing worthwhile work.

Positive Internal Factors

1. Feeling good about yourself (high self-esteem).

2. Feeling confident and empowered.

3. Pushing your level of accomplishment.

4. Sensing achievement and recognition.

5. Feeling positive about your work.

6. Feeling rewarded.

Creating a welcoming office space can *increase* positive attitude.

OVERCOMING LOW SELF-ESTEEM

Low self-esteem is one of the major causes of a negative attitude. You may have had an influential person in your past—a parent, teacher, or sibling—whose messages invalidated you. Now you carry those messages in your head and invalidate yourself with negative self-talk. People with low self-esteem have little respect for themselves. They:

1. Feel alone and disconnected from others.
2. Feel inferior or think they have little worth or no unique abilities.
3. Feel helpless and lack confidence in their ability to change their lives.
4. Blame others or circumstances for their lives.
5. Are vulnerable to negative peer pressure.
6. Are at higher risk for drug and alcohol abuse.
7. Are at higher risk for eating disorders, crime, and suicide.
8. Are often intolerant and critical of people who are different.
9. Are often fearful of change.

4

10. Do not work well with others.

11. Focus on externals (appearance, clothes, material things).

12. Tend to be quiet and avoid speaking their minds.

A positive attitude starts with a sense of self-worth. When you have high self-esteem, you appreciate, respect, and believe in yourself, and you feel worthwhile. You know that, deep down, you have the ability, inner strength, and confidence to handle change and adapt to life. People with high self-esteem:

1. Like and trust themselves.

2. Make friends easily.

3. Are cooperative and work well with others.

4. Take pride in their work and achievements.

5. Are creative and make sound decisions.

6. Are enthusiastic about their jobs and lives.

7. Are confident and self-directed.

8. Feel that they are connected to others.

9. Feel unique.

10. Feel empowered to take control of their lives.

11. Feel that they are responsible for their actions.

12. Celebrate the differences in people.

Exercise 4.3: How Is Your Self-Esteem?

1. Do you like working with your co-workers? Do you feel as if you belong to a business team? Explain. _____
_____
_____
_____

2. What makes you a unique person at work? What special talents do you offer the company? _____

_____

_____

_____

3. In what ways do you have control over your worklife? _____

_____

_____

_____

4. How do you demonstrate that you are responsible for your behavior at work. _____

_____

_____

_____

Building Your Self-Esteem

Below are just some of the many ways you can build your self-esteem:

1. Discover and develop unique talents.
2. Continually learn new skills.
3. Affirm what is working in your life.
4. Use discipline and persistence to meet your goals.
5. Create a sense of community with your co-workers.
6. Practice integrity, civility, and respect with everyone.
7. Start looking for the good in people and situations.
8. Reframe problems as challenges and opportunities.
9. Review and build on daily successes.
10. Reprogram your mind with positive thoughts.
11. Associate with and model people with high self-esteem.
12. Respect your body, mind, and time.

13. Cross off items that you complete on your "To Do" list.

14. Reward yourself for reaching goals.

15. Contribute your time and talents to your community.

OVERCOMING FEARS

The Fear of Failure

Have you had the experience of trying something new or challenging, being afraid that you would fail, and wishing you had a burst of energy and confidence? Do you wish you could sharpen your focus, get your adrenaline going, think clearer, and be more alert? Fear of failure often works *against* you. Think about a time when you were in a sporting event or had to give a speech. It wasn't the event that made you fearful but the *thought* of the event. The same fear that gives you butterflies in your stomach, makes your heart beat fast, and causes an increase in your breathing also gives you a positive boost of energy. Fear is not reality; it is an emotion that you can experience and overcome. Learn to channel the rush of fear into a focused drive to excel in a new and stressful situation.

The Fear of Success

Have you noticed that many people set goals and then promptly go about sabotaging them with negative attitudes and actions? A co-worker may enroll in a seminar to learn new job skills and then cut classes, avoid studying, and feel discouraged that he failed. Another friend may work hard to get a much-wanted job then miss several days of work, get into petty arguments at the office, and quickly feel the work is "boring." Just as some people must work at overcoming their fear of failure, others must overcome their fear of success. If their self-images say they are failures, they tend to act out that script. This results in a self-fulfilling prophecy of failure. They wish for success, they say they want success, but they may subconsciously sabotage themselves. Learn to observe your thoughts and behaviors toward success.

Some people question whether they have worked hard enough or paid enough dues to have good things. They feel guilty being happy in a world full of misery. Remind yourself that you will not make the world a better place by thinking and behaving in a negative manner. You can be realistic about problems and still be positive. In fact, very few advances have been made in life by focusing on the negative. You must see the possibilities in order to make positive changes.

> **Tip**
>
> Have a motivational speaker come to your workplace and discuss topics such as self-esteem, fear, perception, and attitude. Schedule the meeting for an hour or two during work times and have coffee and doughnuts. This meeting should be low-keyed and fun with plenty of time to discuss and interact.

4

OVERCOMING FAULTY PERCEPTIONS

Faulty perception is a major cause of poor work attitudes. Perception, or how you see and interpret events, is directly tied to how you see yourself and how you communicate with others. Your attitude is influenced by your perception of the world. You may recall observing how different people see the same person or event in an entirely different way. All people tend to think that what they see is the truth. Most people, however, have mental maps of what the world should be or what they want it to be, instead of how it really is. In a sense, you filter out what you don't want to see. These perceptual filters determine your attitude toward people and events. Here are just a few of the more common perceptual filters:

1. Snap judgments. Everyone is guilty of making judgments before all the facts are in. Think over the times you made up your mind about a person or situation before acquiring relevant information or facts.

2. Projection. This is the tendency to project your feelings onto another person. You might be ambitious and strive to win promotions. You project this belief onto others. If they don't share your ambition, you may believe that they are lazy. Think back to a time when you projected your feelings onto someone else.

3. Stereotyping. A common perceptual filter is stereotyping a whole group as a result of negative experiences you may have had with one or two people. Some of the strongest stereotypes involve racial groups or gender.

4. Generalization. Generalization is an exaggeration of a small part of the truth. You may turn in a report late, but that does not mean you are lazy or stupid. It is important not to generalize a problem or situation or to exaggerate your personal flaws or inadequacies based on one incident.

Critical Thinking Strategies

Although no one sees the world with absolute clarity or complete objectivity, it is important to become a critical thinker in order to make sound judgments and decisions. Try these strategies:

1. Ask pertinent questions and gather necessary facts and information.
2. Compare beliefs, assumptions, and opinions with facts.
3. Actively listen and give feedback.
4. Respect others and treat each person as a unique human being.
5. Engage in thinking that is conscientious, logical, and purposeful.

Tip

Assign the role of critical thinker to various people during meetings. Rotate this role so everyone gets a chance to develop skills in this area. After discussions, point out that people see things differently and that often these perceptions are influenced by attitudes.

Chapter 4 Checkpoints

✓ Barriers to a positive attitude include low self-esteem, fear, and faulty perceptions.

✓ People with high self-esteem:
   Like and trust others.
   Discover and develop their unique talents.
   Continue to learn new skills.
   Build teamwork with their co-workers.

✓ Critical thinking skills include gathering facts and pertinent information and separating beliefs, assumptions, and opinions from facts.

5 | Creating Positive Work Attitudes

This chapter will help you to:

- Recognize that attitude is a choice.
- Reframe difficult situations.
- Use positive self-talk and imagery.
- Set and support your goals.
- Reward yourself when you develop a new positive attitude.
- Create positive attitude patterns.
- Model positive behavior.

Lynn Carter had just been hired as a copyeditor at a publishing house. She was very excited about her new job, but the first day she was confronted by several co-workers who warned her about their boss, John Bishler. They described his temper, his shouting, and his perfectionist view. Lynn decided to use this information to make the best of her new job. She was careful with her editing and prompt in her assignments. Several weeks later, however, John called her into the office and yelled at her for making a minor mistake. Her first reaction was anger, but she remained calm and professional and told him she would talk to him at the end of the day. Lynn went back to her office to plan her meeting with John. ■

Questions to Consider

1. What would you advise Lynn to do to prepare for her meeting with John? _____

_____

_____

_____

2. What could Lynn do that would help her choose a positive work attitude? _____

_____

_____

_____

5

CHOOSE A POSITIVE ATTITUDE

The first step in changing is to realize that you do have the power to change. You are not a victim of life, but a person who is in charge of your emotions and thoughts. It is clear that no one but you can make you feel inferior, foolish, incompetent, angry, or negative. Take full responsibility for your attitudes. You can change any attitude that does not work for you. Healthy habits are created in the same way that unhealthy habits are—by repeated practice.

In Chapter 4, you described a time when you were motivated and positive. If you have been positive once in your life, you can re-create this state. The way to start is to see things differently.

REFRAME THE SITUATION

Why is it that some people, who seem to have everything, complain endlessly about being victims, while other people who face enormous obstacles and loss, live their lives with joy, optimism, and inner peace? Part of the answer lies in the ability to reframe. How you see a situation will determine the action you take. Reframing is taking a situation and choosing to see it in a new light.

In the chapter-opening vignette, Lynn chose to reframe her situation to make it work for her. She planned for her meeting with John by focusing on the positive aspects of his personality and determining how she could best work with him. Their story continues:

After work, Lynn entered John's office feeling confident and secure. She told John how much she appreciated his candor and straightforward manner. Lynn explained that she had worked for supervisors who saved their concerns for the performance review. She was grateful that her relationship with John could be open and above-board. John had never had a co-worker respond in such a calm and professional manner. He apologized for getting angry, and Lynn and John went on to have a very rewarding, professional, and productive working relationship. ∎

Lynn wasn't just using positive thinking; she was putting the situation in the best possible context, learning from the experience, and moving forward with positive action.

Exercise 5.1: Reframing a Situation

Imagine that you are working your way through school by working part-time at a fast-food restaurant. You find the work boring and demanding with little room for creativity or individual thought. This could be a pretty dreary way to spend 20 hours of your week. How can you reframe the situation? _____
_____
_____

You could reframe this situation by looking at the basic skills you are learning that can be transferred to any job. You are learning to be on time, take orders, be friendly to customers, work well with other people, observe how your boss solves problems and makes decisions, and so on.

■ **Exercise 5.2: Reframing Your Challenging Situations**

Identify several situations in your life that are bothering you or that you consider challenging. List several different ways to reframe these situations.

_____	_____
_____	_____
_____	_____

USE POSITIVE SELF-TALK

Throughout the ages, many religious leaders, philosophers, and writers have stressed the power of thought and self-talk. Your behavior is the result of your self-image and the thoughts and words you use to describe yourself and situations. When you use positive self-talk, you make it more likely that your outer life will become positive too.

■ **Exercise 5.3: Self-talk**

Write down the words you use to describe yourself and your actions at work. Which ones are positive and encouraging and which ones are negative and discouraging? Some examples follow:

_____

_____

_____

Positive Self-talk

I can finish this report on time.

I can learn any new skill.

I will make the best of this situation.

Negative Self-talk

I am always late for meetings.

I am not good with budgets.

This job is hopeless.

USE POSITIVE IMAGERY

Imagery is vividly visualizing yourself behaving in certain ways in certain situations. Positive people imagine themselves in a positive light and clearly see themselves successfully producing the results they want. Imagery is a powerful tool for increasing confidence and motivation and creating positive work attitudes.

Several times during the week, focus on your images. Are you seeing yourself successful, are you expecting and visualizing wonderful outcomes to events, or do you fear the worst? Do you project fearful, unpleasant situations? When you daydream, do you allow yourself to think of creative,

glorious days or do you stop yourself from daydreaming and tell yourself you are foolish?

■ Exercise 5.4: Imagery

Imagine that you want to change your attitude about your job and feel more confident, especially about your ability to control budget planning in your job. Visualize yourself in detail as a successful, confident person. Notice your relaxed state of mind, your calm and forceful gestures, your use of direct eye contact. Notice the professional image you project. See this image become bigger, clearer, and closer. Conjure up a positive self-image, use positive self-talk, and use positive imagery to bring you closer to reaching your desired state. Some examples follow.

Self-image:

"My image of myself is of a confident, competent person. I am confident working with budgets and figures. I have control over my personal and professional life."

Self-talk:

"I am a competent person."
"I like to do financial planning."
"I am in control of my job."

Imagery:

"I see myself working on budgets and attending financial meetings. I see myself walking with confidence and poise."

SET AND SUPPORT YOUR GOALS

Setting and supporting your goals is another way to increase your self-esteem, improve your attitude, and increase your productivity.

■ Exercise 5.5: Supporting Your Goals

Choose one work goal that you have been unable to achieve. If you were advising someone else on the best way to achieve this goal, what attitude, self-talk, and behavior would you recommend that would produce the desired results? How would you make certain the new behavior endured?

Goal:

_____

_____

Attitude:

_____

_____

Self-talk:

_____

_____

Behavior:

_____

_____

Now consider the barriers that have prevented you from reaching your goal and identify any available resources that can help you. An example of an internal resource might be your own creativity; an example of an external resource might be a support group.

REWARD YOURSELF

Whenever you develop a new positive attitude or behavior, you must reinforce it. You must clearly associate your new attitude with pleasure, and focus on the benefits of the change. The better you can associate the new attitude with feelings of pleasure and accomplishment, the greater your commitment to continue this change.

Suppose you want to get to work earlier and accomplish more during your morning hours. The following list suggests ways to reinforce your behavior when you reach your new goal:

1. **Acknowledge and accept praise from others.** "Thank you. I feel good about accomplishing this task before 10 AM."

2. **Acknowledge and accept praise from yourself.** "I like how it feels when I am more productive. I like the benefits of increased productivity."

3. **Acknowledge and praise others.** "John, you have such a positive attitude. Thanks for exploring new alternatives to the publication problem. I really appreciated your creativity."

4. **Reward yourself often:**
   - Take a walk at lunch.
   - Give yourself a break with the best coffee or tea.
   - Have lunch with a co-worker.
   - Read a professional journal.
   - Decorate your office.
   - Buy yourself new office equipment.
   - Wear a great-looking professional outfit.
   - Attend a seminar.

CREATE POSITIVE ATTITUDE PATTERNS

Look back over your day. You get up, brush your teeth, take a shower, get dressed, drink coffee, and go to work. Some patterns are positive and some are negative. For example, what thoughts go through your mind when you wake up for work? Do you find yourself saying, "Oh no, not another day at work," or does your subconscious mind say, "I can't wait to start the day"?

■ Exercise 5.6: Negative and Positive Patterns

1. What are some negative patterns in your life? Explain. (Examples might include, "I'm always broke," or, "I always work with difficult people.") _____

_____

_____

2. What are some positive patterns in your life? Explain. (Examples might include, "I'm always healthy," or, "I always follow through.") _____

   _____

   _____

How do you change patterns and negative habits or attitudes that are getting in the way of your success? The answer that runs through this book is that your behavior will change—indeed, your life will change—when your attitude changes. You are not stuck with negative habits or patterns. As you learned in Chapter 1, your self-image has a major influence on your behavior. Your self-image determines how much you will accomplish at work and how you view your job and your co-workers. In a sense, the world mirrors your self-image. It is important, therefore, to change the way you think and talk about yourself and your job. A positive self-image allows you to focus on your job successes and to respect yourself and others.

People often want to make lots of changes quickly and feel discouraged if they experience setbacks. Lasting change is most effective, however, when you choose one habit that you want to change and work on it consistently for a month. It takes about 30 days to change a habit. Recognize your patterns and give yourself time to change them. Be consistent, patient, and persistent and expect positive results. Work on only one attitude change at a time. The following formula for change can help you:

1. Acknowledge your old pattern of thinking and behaving.
2. Choose a new positive habit.
3. Create an action plan to reach your new goal.
4. Practice your new habit for one month.
5. Reward yourself: associate pleasure with your new habit.
6. Assess where you are after one month and readjust as necessary.

> ### ■ Tip
>
> Be your own best friend. Make yourself an inspiring tape of your favorite songs. Tape daily affirmations on your mirror. These may include:
>
> I am a worthwhile person.
>
> I choose to be positive and happy today.
>
> I am confident and calm.
>
> I have the resources to handle any situation.
>
> I am disciplined and persistent in reaching my goals.
>
> I break down large tasks into manageable challenges.
>
> I like myself, my job, and my life.
>
> I see change as an opportunity to grow.

5

MODEL POSITIVE PEOPLE

Have you ever been with someone who is negative and found your attitude and mood becoming negative? Positive attitudes are contagious, too. To create a positive attitude, model people who are positive and productive. They will bring out the best in you. You may be tempted to think that positive people are just lucky. They are not. Motivated, successful people are just like you, only they have learned to control their thoughts and actions, work with more persistance, and believe in themselves. Successful people get discouraged too, but they know how to get off dead center. They are committed to their goals, and this vision helps them succeed. Observe positive people. Identify what it is about them that makes them positive and emulate those characteristics.

Chapter 5 Checkpoints

✓ Empower yourself to choose a positive attitude.

✓ Use the power of reframing.

✓ Use positive self-talk to reprogram your attitude.

✓ Imagine yourself being successful.

✓ Reward yourself.

✓ Use the power of setting goals.

✓ Focus on the positive.

✓ Change your negative attitude patterns.

✓ Model positive people.

6 | A Supportive Work Climate

This chapter will help you to:

- Define work climate.
- Identify the factors that make up a positive work climate.
- Identify the factors that make up a negative work climate.
- Identify strategies to create a supportive work climate.
- Assess whether your reward system creates a positive or negative work climate.

Alfonso Ramiriz, a longtime production supervisor for a toy company, is sitting in his office reflecting on his recent performance review. He received a good overall rating, but his boss remarked that Alfonso should be more open to change and should create a more positive work climate.

On the following Tuesday, supervisors are to meet with top management to discuss some major organizational changes. Each supervisor is to prepare a plan to meet new budget cutbacks, to deal with a new product line, and to help staff through this difficult transition.

Alfonso comes from the traditional school of management; he believes that people should work hard and get their rewards from a job well done. He has never thought much about creating a positive work climate. In fact, he believes it is important to keep his distance from his co-workers. But given his performance review, he knows he needs to focus on the positive factors of the changes and to create a supportive atmosphere for his department. ■

Questions to Consider

1. What would you advise Alfonso to do to prepare for this meeting?

   _____

   _____

   _____

2. How can Alfonso create a more positive work climate during this time of change? _____

   _____

   _____

   _____

6

THE WORK CLIMATE

Just as people have attitudes, so do organizations. Every organization has a climate or corporate culture that reflects the attitudes and values of the people who work there. Climate is the verbal and nonverbal communication that occurs in the office. Individual thoughts, attitudes, and behaviors can create either a positive or negative climate. How the business is conducted is another major factor in establishing an office climate. The arrangement of office furniture, clothing, and office rules also can set a tone. A positive work climate supports and is sensitive to the well-being of its employees. It rewards people for working together, for quality work, for positive attitudes, and for creative thinking.

A positive work climate does not just happen. It takes effort, practice, awareness, and knowledge to reduce misunderstandings and conflict and to improve work relationships and productivity and build a sense of community. The following lists will help you understand the factors that create a positive or negative climate.

A Positive Work Climate

A positive and productive work climate is created when you:

1. **Describe the problem.** Gather factual information.
2. **Give positive feedback.** Look for what's right. Give positive reinforcement, praise, and encouragement.
3. **Respect others.**
4. **Are an active listener.** Listen with understanding and empathy.
5. **Are open-minded.** Explore new ideas and solutions.
6. **Are problem-centered.** Focus on solving the problem, not on the personality. Ask, "What is the problem?" not, "Who is to blame?"
7. **Are fully in the present.** Focus on the present, not the past. Ask, "What can be done?" not, "Why did this happen?"
8. **Give high visibility to others.** Offer assignments, make introductions, and highlight good work.
9. **Build confidence.** Create opportunities for speaking, presentations, training, and development.
10. **Build rapport.** Nonverbal communication is warm, friendly, supportive, and accepting.
11. **Are polite.** Use good business etiquette and value people as part of the office community.

A Negative Work Climate

A negative and unproductive work climate is created when you:

1. **Use judgmental speech.** Evaluate and judge people.
2. **Give negative feedback.** Criticize behavior; look for what is wrong.
3. **Act superior.** Focus on the use of power, titles, and status.
4. **Are controlling.** Disregard the other person's feelings or point of view.

5. **Have dogmatic views.** Close yourself off to new ideas or solutions.

6. **Don't allow mistakes.** Focus on blame and fault-finding.

7. **Focus on the past.** Create a self-fulfilling prophecy based on rigid views of people and situations.

8. **Withhold feedback.** Don't give feedback or information. Don't allow people to be visible. Keep expectations unclear.

9. **Invalidate confidence.** Offer little opportunity for growth and participation.

10. **Keep aloof and distant.** Give little nonverbal communication. Remain neutral and give noncaring messages.

11. **Focus on competition and separatism.** Believe that it's a dog-eat-dog world and that it is best not to get too personally involved with co-workers.

6

Tip

Give criticism judiciously, gracefully, and always in private. Treat all people with respect and never stoop to yelling, name-calling, gossip, or sarcasm. Take people out for a cup of coffee or a walk and gently discuss the situation. Ask for their response and suggestions before you give yours.

Exercise 6.1: Work Climate

Look at the work climate in your department. Would you describe it as basically positive or negative? _____

_____

_____

1. List several positive factors.

_____

_____

2. List several negative factors.

_____

_____

STRATEGIES THAT WORK

What can you do to create a more supportive climate? Ask yourself the following questions. Your answers will demonstrate how far you need to go to achieve a supportive climate.

1. Do you describe a person's behavior or ask for information about a situation, or do you tend to be judgmental? (For example, do you say something like, "You were late for the staff meetings three times this month," or do you say, "You are rude and inconsiderate to barge in late for the meetings"?)

2. Do you focus on the problem and solutions, or do you try to control and influence the behavior of the other person?

3. Are you free of strategy and focused in the present, or do you send a double message and try to gain power?

4. Do you convey empathy and respect for the other person's feelings, or do you behave as if you don't care?

5. Do you convey mutual trust and respect, or do you behave in a superior manner that makes the other person feel inferior?

6. Are you open to new ideas, solutions, and ideas, or are you dogmatic and act as if you have all the answers?

Tip

Praise your co-workers. Recognizing good work is important throughout the year and means more if it comes from various co-workers rather than from just the supervisor or as a bonus check once a year. Look for the good in others and search out things to praise. Make certain you recognize the president of the company, top administrators, and entry-level staff. Everyone responds to praise.

How to Create a Climate That Respects the Dignity of All Workers

1. Learn to be an active listener.
2. Create a bond with others.
3. Treat everyone with respect and courtesy.
4. Be consistent and fair.
5. Remember the golden rule.
6. Don't gossip or spread rumors.
7. Make a conscious decision to be responsible for your actions.

How to Create an Ethical Climate

1. If your first instinct or impression tells you something is wrong, it probably is.
2. Imagine that your mother, spouse, or child were standing in the room. Would your actions or language be acceptable?
3. If a reporter were writing your situation into a story to put on the front page of the newspaper, how would it sound? Could you justify your actions?
4. Before doing something that is questionable, ask yourself, "Is this action worth losing my job or destroying my relationship?"
5. If your child were to ask you if this situation were ethical, how would you respond?

How to Create a Climate That Celebrates Diversity

1. Celebrate, don't just tolerate, differences.
2. Create harmony through trust and respect.
3. Use employees from different cultures and gender to strengthen a working team.

ASSESS YOUR REWARD SYSTEM

A basic management principle states that what an organization rewards will continue. This reward system is part of the work climate. Despite what the organization's written goals, philosophy, or mission statement says, it is what is rewarded every day that creates the real work climate. Look around your workplace and observe what is being rewarded.

■ Exercise 6.2: What Does Your Company Reward?

Does your company or office reward:

1. Teamwork or individual stars?
2. Activity or productivity?
3. Cooperation or competition?
4. The status quo or new ideas?
5. Risk taking or risk avoidance (by penalizing unsuccessful risks)?
6. Real solutions or quick fixes?
7. Loyalty or no job security?
8. Open communication or the rumor mill?
9. Harmony or office conflicts?
10. Streamlined paperwork or complicated red tape?

Once you decide what attitudes and behaviors you want your workplace to reflect, you can set up a reward system that will create and transform your work climate.

Chapter 6 Checkpoints

✓ Work climates reflect the attitudes and values of the people who work in the organization.

✓ A positive climate:
  Is problem centered.
  Gives positive feedback.
  Is respectful, civil, and polite.
  Is open-minded.
  Encourages active listening.
  Builds confidence.
  Creates rapport.
  Enhances visibility.

✓ A negative climate:
  Is judgmental.
  Gives negative feedback.
  Is dogmatic.
  Invalidates others.

✓ A company's reward system will help determine whether the work climate is positive or negative.

7 | Maintaining Your Positive Attitude

This chapter will help you to:

- Understand the importance of maintaining a positive attitude.
- Identify attitude maintenance strategies.

Luke Geyzinski is a sales representative for a software development company. He is a hard worker, very ambitious, committed to his career, and eager to advance into management. He regularly assesses his strengths and weaknesses, sets goals, and attends several seminars a year on self-improvement and management topics. When he returns from a seminar, he is excited about jumping in and making changes. For a few weeks, he is inspired and works on adopting new strategies, but then reality and day-to-day demands set in and he finds it difficult to maintain a positive attitude and any sense of enthusiasm.

Luke works long hours, leaving him little time for his personal life. He is overweight and out of shape. He feels that he has little time to exercise or eat properly. He resents not spending more time with his family and feeling too exhausted at the end of the day to get involved in community events or hobbies. ∎

Question to Consider

How can Luke create a sense of balance in his life, reduce his stress, and renew his attitude on a regular basis? _____

_____

_____

_____

STAY POSITIVE

It is difficult to have positive work attitudes if your mind and body are out of balance and exhausted. It is essential that you learn to balance your life and increase and focus your energy. Everyone needs to refresh and restore their positive attitudes. Maintenance time is important on a daily basis; it should not be relegated to the confines of an annual vacation.

STRATEGIES FOR STAYING ON TOP

People who have positive work attitudes say they build in daily time to boost their energy and their attitude. Some people like to drive a different way to work occasionally as a way to renew their sense of creativity. Others like to take mini-vacations by closing their eyes several times during their workday and imagining their favorite retreats. They may see themselves at the ocean or relaxing in the sand. Several more strategies follow.

Increase Energy Gains

The tendency to appear overworked, scattered, and emotionally over-loaded with responsibilities is a liability if you want to climb the organizational ladder. Part of projecting a professional and competent image is demonstrating that you have the ability to handle stress, while remaining poised and self-assured.

Here are some suggestions for keeping your energy up:

1. Eat healthy meals. You cannot have a positive attitude if you are undernourished or hungry. Always eat a good breakfast. Bring fruit, nuts, or whole grain muffins to eat with your morning tea or coffee break.

2. Get extra sleep. Everything looks better after a good night's sleep. Experts say that many people suffer from sleep deprivation. This can result in a poor attitude, low energy, and lack of productivity. Try going to bed at a regular time every night and getting enough rest so that you wake naturally without an alarm, feeling rested and ready for the day.

3. Exercise regularly. Exercise increases your energy and overall stamina. Aerobic exercise produces endorphins that increase your sense of well-being.

4. Meditate and use positive imagery. You can become very relaxed and increase your energy by vividly rehearsing success. By breathing deeply and focusing on positive images, your heartbeat and breathing become relaxed and rhythmic.

Eliminate Energy Drains

It is equally important to eliminate those behaviors and mental activities that drain your energy. Here are some common energy drains that sap your strength and reduce your productivity. Can you think of more?

1. Excessive alcohol (alcohol is a depressant).
2. Nicotine and other drugs (nicotine is a depressant).
3. Overeating and an unhealthy diet.
4. Too little sleep.
5. Worrying about the future.
6. Procrastination.
7. Reliving sad experiences and focusing on losses.
8. Maintaining an unorganized and dull work space.
9. Working without taking breaks.
10. Watching television for hours at a time.

Create Balance in Your Life

At various times in your life, it is important and necessary to put in extra effort and work long hours. A project deadline must be met or a crisis must be dealt with. When a time frame is established, you can see the end in sight and know that you have the energy reserves to keep going for a short time. It is vital, however, that you take time after the big push to recharge your energy and get your life back in balance.

■ Exercise 7.1: Reassess Your Life

Reassess the areas of your life that you have ignored or that are out of balance. Identify the goals that you have for each area and consider whether you spend an appropriate amount of time on each one:

	Area	*Goals*
1.	Family.	_____
2.	Health.	_____
3.	Spiritual life.	_____
4.	Career.	_____
5.	Education and training.	_____
6.	Relationships.	_____
7.	Finances.	_____
8.	Time for self.	_____
9.	Home.	_____
10.	Community.	_____
11.	Personal growth.	_____
12.	Other.	_____

Listen to Your Body

Your body often sends you wake-up calls when your life is out of balance. Pain is one such message. Some headaches are in this category. What excuses do you give yourself for not addressing the underlying causes (assuming that external causes are ruled out) of headache pain?

Burnout is excessive stress that has accumulated and has a negative effect on your attitude and body. Some common signs of burnout are:

1. Migraine headaches.
2. Backache.
3. Worry.
4. Sleep disturbances.
5. High blood pressure.

A positive attitude can reduce tension, improve digestion, and contribute to overall mental and physical well-being. Positive thoughts can contribute to a healthy body, and negative thoughts and emotions can create stress and tension. In general, positive people suffer fewer illnesses and recover from them faster than negative people.

7

T i p

Keep your agreements. Everyone appreciates people who keep their word. If you say you are going to do something, do it. Write down assignments so you won't forget them.

Bring a Sense of Worth, Confidence, and Purpose to Your Job

It is important to genuinely like your work. Your job should match your personality, values, intelligence, and skills. It is important to feel that you are working to improve the world and to feel that you are part of a team. If you feel that your job is a mismatch or that it lacks integrity, you might consider changing your career. Sometimes, however, you may just need to look at the larger picture. Positive people realize that even the smallest task is important for the organization; they are able to look beyond the unpleasant parts of any job.

Spend time reinforcing and nourishing your sense of worth. This nourishment creates more success; you are able to form stronger work relationships, you expect more out of your job, you set higher job performance standards, and you work to make a difference.

■ Exercise 7.2: What Is Your Value to Your Organization?

How does your role in the organization fit into the organization's overall mission? In what way does your job performance enhance the organization's image and the quality of customer service? _____
_____
_____
_____
_____

Make Being Positive a Daily Habit

Find ways to build daily habits into your life that refresh your body, mind, and spirit. Here are a few suggestions:

1. Take a 15-minute break with a co-worker mid-morning.
2. Work with others on projects.
3. Go to work early once or twice a week and read a professional article.
4. Climb stairs or walk reports around the office whenever possible.
5. Keep a funny file in your desk of humorous office jokes, memos, and stories.
6. Take a walk at lunch with another co-worker—don't talk about business.
7. Take time to project a professional image that makes you feel good.
8. Wake up early and write a few letters to friends, do yoga, or read an inspirational biography of a person you admire.
9. Create an organized and inspiring work space.
10. Look at office problems as interesting puzzles or games to solve. Approach them as a child would creatively approach a game.

Chapter 7 Checkpoints

✓ Strategies for staying on top of a good attitude include daily minivacations and teamwork.

✓ Energy increasers include healthful eating, exercise, extra rest, and relaxation.

✓ Energy drains include excessive alcohol, nicotine and other drugs, overeating, poor diet, too little sleep, and few interests or hobbies.

Post-Test

Now that you have reviewed and practiced the strategies and tips outlined in this book, it is time to reinforce your learning by taking this post-test.

1. Why is a positive self-image essential for a positive attitude?

2. What are the characteristics of a person with a positive attitude?

3. What is the most fundamental human need?

4. List at least four positive work attitudes with a brief description of each.

5. List at least four negative work attitudes and at least one suggestion for counteracting each one.

6. What are several characteristics of a person with high self-esteem?

7. What are the steps in reframing a situation?

8. How can positive self-talk and imagery work to create a positive attitude? Give an example.

9. List at least three strategies for creating a positive attitude.

10. What is a supportive work climate?

11. Identify at least four ways that you can maintain your positive attitude.

The Business Skills Express Series

This growing series of books addresses a broad range of key business skills and topics to meet the needs of employees, human resource departments, and training consultants.

To obtain information about these and other Business Skills Express books, please call Irwin Professional Publishing toll free at: 1-800-634-3966.

Effective Performance Management
ISBN   1-55623-867-3

Hiring the Best
ISBN   1-55623-865-7

Writing that Works
ISBN   1-55623-856-8

Customer Service Excellence
ISBN   1-55623-969-6

Writing for Business Results
ISBN   1-55623-854-1

Powerful Presentation Skills
ISBN   1-55623-870-3

Meetings that Work
ISBN   1-55623-866-5

Effective Teamwork
ISBN   1-55623-880-0

Time Management
ISBN   1-55623-888-6

Assertiveness Skills
ISBN   1-55623-857-6

Motivation at Work
ISBN   1-55623-868-1

Overcoming Anxiety at Work
ISBN   1-55623-869-X

Positive Politics at Work
ISBN   1-55623-879-7

Telephone Skills at Work
ISBN   1-55623-858-4

Managing Conflict at Work
ISBN   1-55623-890-8

The New Supervisor: Skills for Success
ISBN   1-55623-762-6

**The *Americans with Disabilities Act:*
What Supervisors Need to Know**
ISBN   1-55623-889-4

**Managing the Demands of
Work and Home**
ISBN   0-7863-0221-6

Effective Listening Skills
ISBN   0-7863-0102-4

Goal Management at Work
ISBN   0-7863-0225-9

Positive Attitudes at Work
ISBN   0-7863-0100-8

Supervising the Difficult Employee
ISBN   0-7863-0219-4

Cultural Diversity in the Workplace
ISBN   0-7863-0125-2

Managing Change in the Workplace
ISBN   0-7863-0162-7

Negotiating for Business Results
ISBN   0-7863-0114-7

Practical Business Communication
ISBN   0-7863-0227-5

High Performance Speaking
ISBN   0-7863-0222-4

Delegation Skills
ISBN   0-7863-0105-9

Coaching Skills: a Guide for Supervisors
ISBN   0-7863-0220-8

Customer Service and the Telephone
ISBN   0-7863-0224-0

Creativity at Work
ISBN   0-7863-0223-2

Effective Interpersonal Relationships
ISBN   0-7863-0255-0

The Participative Leader
ISBN   0-7863-0252-6

Building Customer Loyalty
ISBN   0-7863-0253-4

Getting and Staying Organized
ISBN   0-7863-0254-2

Total Quality Selling
ISBN   0-7863-0324-7

Business Etiquette
ISBN   0-7863-0323-9

Empowering Employees
ISBN   0-7863-0314-X

Training Skills for Supervisors
ISBN   0-7863-0313-1

Moving Meetings
ISBN   0-7863-0333-6

Multicultural Customer Service
ISBN   0-7863-0332-8

Printed in the United States
21345LVS00005B/139-760